No. 6

DEPARTMENT OF DOCKS AND FERRIES
Pier "A," North River
NEW YORK CITY

REPORT

ACCOMPANYING

Submission of Plans for an Elevated Freight Railroad Connecting Manhattan Terminals

AT THE

Port of New York

SUBMITTED BY

CALVIN TOMKINS

Commissioner of Docks

JANUARY 26, 1911

Brooklyn Eagle Press
1911

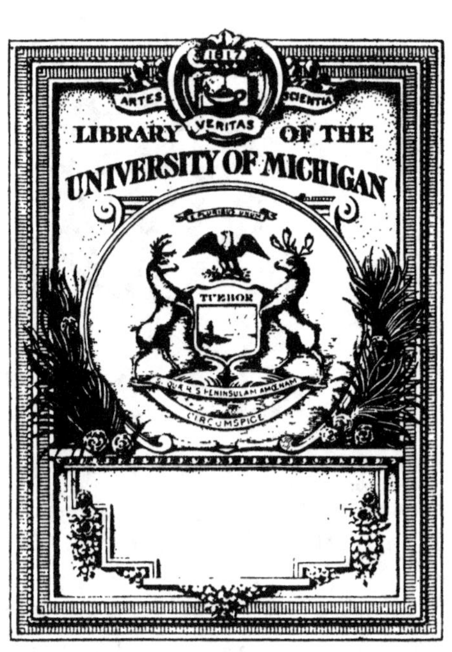
1817
ARTES
VERITAS
SCIENTIA
LIBRARY OF THE
UNIVERSITY OF MICHIGAN
TUEBOR
CIRCUMSPICE

DEPARTMENT OF DOCKS AND FERRIES
Pier "A," North River
NEW YORK CITY

REPORT

ACCOMPANYING

Submission of Plans for an Elevated Freight Railroad Connecting Manhattan Terminals

AT THE

Port of New York

SUBMITTED BY

CALVIN TOMKINS

Commissioner of Docks

JANUARY 26, 1911

HON. WILLIAM J. GAYNOR,

Mayor, and Chairman of the Board of Estimate and Apportionment.

SIR—I have reported to you under date of July, 1910; November 21, 1910, and December 16, 1910, on the desirability of providing under City auspices, a series of west side railroad terminals connected by a marginal elevated road between the New York Central yard at Sixtieth street and Washington market. I shall not rehearse at length the reasons cited in my former reports for the conclusions which I have reached, except to briefly summarize the more important of them. This report can be intelligently read and considered only as the last of the above noted series.

I include in this report several drawings which are tentative studies of the proposed terminal, and of the elevated railroad and float bridges. I have prepared models and photographs showing existing conditions, and also the suggested installations. These I am prepared to submit to your Honor and to the Board of Estimate and Apportionment.

The plan permits of the terminal utilization of marginal lands owned or leased by the New York Central and other railroad companies, and I believe affords the only comprehensive solution possible for the present waterfront congestion below Twenty-third street, and the prevention of future congestion in the district farther north. It permits of indefinite terminal expansion by the railroads—individualistic use of terminal buildings and float bridges, and joint use of the connecting elevated railroad. It assumes that the railroad companies themselves will secure sites for terminal buildings adjacent to and along the line of the proposed elevated road. Its adoption will ultimately make possible the release for marine purposes of waterfront now used for the daily storage of car floats. These several ends are made possible by transferring cars from floats to the east side of the river street, there to be unloaded and loaded. The ship must go to the dock; the car *can* be taken into a terminal across the street, and should be so transferred. Finally, when a marginal elevated freight road shall have been built by the City, the New York Central tracks can be removed from the surface of Tenth and Eleventh avenues, and West street. That road, jointly with the several New Jersey roads, should be explicitly assured of permanent unimpeded access to all future waterfront terminals over it. If four tracks shall not be found sufficient for the requirements of participating roads, additional trackage up to at least ten tracks may be provided by the City.

The ultimate consequence of such an overhead installation will be the creation of a double-decked marginal railroad street. In order to keep this street under complete municipal control, and at all times subject to the terminal policy of the City—as regards power to make physical changes necessary to meet changing commercial conditions—the City should build and own the elevated structure, contracting with railroad companies desiring to use it—either separately, or preferably through the medium of a joint terminal company, the organization of which the City should procure, and in the ownership and control of which, the roads, as they seek to use it, should be permitted to participate on terms of equality. This policy will be in accord with the established usages of those American cities which have made the greatest advances in waterfront terminal improvements—especially Montreal, New Orleans and San Francisco. Such an elevated road will of necessity become the dominating factor in the development of the future west side general terminal, and at no time should control over it be permitted to pass away from the City. Every road should be assured of a continuing, unobstructed right of way over it to any terminal it may establish along its line. The adoption of such a policy—which implies the real control of an owner in possession—will be equally advantageous to the City and to all the railroads coming to it, since the entire west side will thus be made accessible to and for each separate road. Interest, maintenance and sinking fund expenses will not be heavy and will be recouped by the City from reasonable rental or service charges, thus promptly placing the improvement in the self-sustaining class, exempt from the debt limit. In short, the City will have created not a debt, but an asset.

Specific Plan.

Construct a four-track elevated freight railroad from Sixtieth street as far south as Fulton street in such a manner that additional tracks may be added and connections made with buildings on the easterly side of the river street. I have shown in drawing "A," one type of structure which may be used and which can readily be added to if necessity arises. The cost of this structure is estimated at $350 per running foot, or for the distance between Sixtieth and Fulton streets, of 23,000 feet, a total of $8,050,000; this amount to include the third rail. It is an open question whether at first it will be best to provide a power house or to buy current from a private corporation. I am of the opinion that the latter will be the better policy until the undertaking shall have assumed sufficiently large proportions to warrant the expenditure necessary for a power plant. If it shall appear desirable to devote Washington market to the purpose of a joint terminal, it is estimated that this improvement may be effected at a cost not to exceed $300,000; this would include the construction of a team truck yard on the street level and a railroad yard on the second level. A building on this plot can be carried above the two railroad levels, renting the overhead space on terms advantageous to the City. When the structure shall have been built, the New York Central Railroad Company should be called upon to remove its tracks from the surface of Tenth and Eleventh avenues and West street. This company already owns several blocks of property between Thirtieth and Thirty-seventh streets admirably adapted for terminal purposes. In addition it will be necessary for it to secure property on West street at or near the intersection with Canal street, to care for the business which is now being conducted at St. John's Park, since the Ninth avenue elevated prevents access by any transverse elevated structure east of the line of Ninth avenue.

Open Twelfth Avenue.

It will be necessary to open Twelfth avenue between Thirty-fourth and Sixtieth streets before a marginal elevated railroad can be built, or any comprehensive west side improvement carried through. Proceedings to open and construct this marginal street should be undertaken without delay. Title to the foot of all the intersecting streets is in the City.

Between Thirty-fourth and Forty-second streets, between Forty-fourth and Forty-ninth streets and between Fifty-eighth and Sixtieth streets, the property is owned by private parties; between Forty-ninth and Fiftieth streets, the City owns 83 feet 10 inches and private parties own 117 feet. These private rights must be acquired either by purchase or by condemnation.

Twelfth avenue has been legally opened to 151st street. Where this avenue has been actually made, it is under the jurisdiction of the President of the Borough of Manhattan, who can remove, or cause to be removed, all obstructions and encumbrances. Where not actually made, the grants to private parties provide that the making of this avenue shall be done by the grantees at their expense. The expense for opening this marginal street is not properly a charge against the elevated railroad, as the waterfront will thereby be made generally available for commercial purposes and the opening will in any event be made in the near future.

Description of Plates.

From the numerous studies which the engineers of this Department have prepared, I have selected and included in this publication the following drawings illustrative of the general features of the plan. The other studies will be submitted in the original drawings.

No. 23, shows a lay-out of the terminal buildings between Twenty-fifth and Thirtieth streets, to which, by means of a loop, access for railroad cars is provided to any of the buildings without passing through other buildings. There is also shown a combination of wide and narrow platforms so that both track floors of the buildings may be used for east and west bound freight. In connection with this plan, provision should be made for direct unloading at the yard between Thirty-eighth and Fortieth streets. This plan, providing as it does for both unloading and loading of cars on each level, will probably minimize the amount of shifting of cars.

No. 25, shows the car storage yard and transfer bridges. This installation shows thirteen transfer bridges and the piers at that location used for the storage of cars as they will be available for no other purpose. The location of the ramp, with reference to the elevated railroad, is also shown, as is the method of connecting with the terminal buildings south of Thirtieth street.

No. 26, shows a lay-out of thirty-six transfer bridges between Thirtieth and Fortieth streets, connected to the elevated railroad by two separate ramps.

No. 28, shows a plan in which by means of ramps, connections can be made from the existing yards of the Baltimore & Ohio Railroad, the Lehigh Valley Railroad, the Erie Railroad and the Pennsylvania Railroad, to the proposed four-track elevated freight railroad. The New York Central yard between Thirtieth and Thirty-seventh streets, can readily and cheaply be similarly connected.

"A," shows a cross-section of the marginal way on which is indicated the proposed four-track elevated freight railroad structure opposite the Chelsea section and in the downtown district, where spur connections can be made to factories and terminal buildings as far east as the Ninth avenue elevated railroad.

St. Louis Terminal Railroad.

Through the courtesy of Mr. William H. Lee, President of the Laclede National Bank of St. Louis, Missouri, I have secured the following information regarding the Terminal Railroad Association of St. Louis.

The Terminal Railroad Association of St. Louis is owned, in equal shares, by fifteen railroads and is operated independently of these fifteen lines. The other roads terminating at St. Louis and East St. Louis receive exactly the same service and accommodations as the proprietary roads, and at exactly the same cost, which insures fair and impartial service for all roads and the patrons of all roads. The tracks of the Terminal Association connect with all lines.

The rates for the service performed are so equalized that all shippers from Terminal rails are on a parity. A shipper on Terminal rails, no matter where located, is on any and all of the roads entering this gateway. The track into his plant and the team yard a block or so away are accessible to any of the roads which he may select. Suppose he is a shipper of small lots of freight; one wagon containing shipments via a dozen or more roads can drive to the Terminal warehouse and discharge the entire load, for the North, East, South and West, and to be shipped via roads whose terminals may be miles apart.

The Terminal Railroad serves as a medium for transferring freight in carloads between the Terminal Yards of the proprietary and tenant roads on the east and those on the west bank of the river, and distributes with its own locomotives, both carload and package freight, to the limits of its rails, in both St. Louis and East St. Louis.

Passenger trains are hauled over the Terminal rails direct to the Union station by the locomotives of the proprietary and tenant lines. Freight trains are received in the yards of the proprietary and tenant lines, where they are broken up and classified for delivery to various destinations. From these yards, the cars are handled by power belonging to the Terminal Railroad Association and the expense of so handling, is prorated on a basis of service performed.

Why Traffic Seeks Manhattan Terminals.

The passenger business of the port flows through lower Manhattan. The same reasons which prompted the Pennsylvania Railroad, at great expense, to establish its Manhattan terminal, are also compelling the passenger and express freight steamers to fix their terminals at Manhattan, where hotels, amusements, wholesale and retail businesses, and railroads are most accessible. High class package freight, and most of the food supply is brought to Manhattan and taken away by the railroads and the steamships, and if delivered elsewhere in the port necessitates long and expensive cartage and ferriage to and from Manhattan. Provision must be made at the docks for the daily reception of food, fuel, building materials and the raw materials for manufacture required by the City; and also for the disposal of ashes, garbage and City wastes and excavated material. At present the handling of the coarser of these commodities involves long hauls. The narrow island of Manhattan is by nature most advantageously placed for receiving and shipping by water, and as a consequence, the internal hauls should be short and cheap. The occupation of so much of the waterfront of the island by railroad car floats interferes with its proper uses for marine commerce. As stated, the cars can be conveyed across the street to be there loaded and unloaded, thus releasing the waterfront for ships and boats.

Conclusion.

The New York Central must elevate its tracks and has already secured sites for terminals above Twenty-third street, adapted for railroad use. If the New Jersey railroads shall not now follow a similar policy in securing inshore terminals, they will be placed at still greater disadvantage than at present in relation to the New York Central. This situation, it is assumed, they will not long be content to remain in. The policy of the railroads, until now, has been to secure, each for itself, needed facilities without regard to others. Proper terminal organization in Manhattan, including a connecting railroad along the west side, can best and quickest be attained through mutual co-operation, but in any event, the City, by anticipating needs, should force the improvement issue. In other words, it should create conditions which shall make it incumbent upon the railroads to fall in with its policy. At present values of real estate along the west side river streets are low, and this temporary condition will facilitate the acquisition of sites and the erection of terminal buildings. The roads which act first will secure the best locations and the cheapest lands.

The City should keep control over present and future physical plans for the development of its terminals, relying upon the Interstate Commerce Commission and the Public Service Commission for regulation of rates and service.

Existing west side defects to be overcome are:

First—Recovery for marine commerce, waterfront now unnecessarily used for the storage of car floats, by transferring cars across the marginal street to be unloaded and loaded there.

Second—Existing disorder and congestion, with its attendant expense, should be terminated and provision made for room to meet the needs of the rapidly expanding railroad and steamship business of Manhattan; incidentally providing berths for sound, river and harbor boats.

Third—The termination of the New York Central surface track nuisance.

The City can compel the removal of the surface tracks, if other means of access shall concurrently be made possible. The Central's plans contemplate the utilization of such an elevated freight road, and I understand that its officials have publicly so stated. The use of the elevated road by the Central will terminate the present parity of disadvantages under which all roads are now operating their terminals. This will compel the other roads to provide terminals in conformity with the City's comprehensive plan.

In closing, I shall anticipate a criticism which will be directed against this report, viz.:

That the City should not at public expense provide an elevated road for the New York Central, which is what that company desires and which the other roads are not asking for, and may not use.

Answer—The City will not build this road for the New York Central, but for itself; in order to maintain its control over all terminals, including those of the New York Central. It will then be in a position continually to make readjustments of terminal needs as required by its expanding commerce and the changing conditions incident to growth. It will also gain the inestimable advantage of making the west side of Manhattan acceptable to all the roads. Subsequently, and as a separate matter, the City will have a choice of alternative policies—either of securing the maximum revenue for its treasury from rentals and service charges; or the minimum revenue necessary to meet interest, maintenance and amortization, and by so doing encourage the more rapid growth of its commerce.

Respectfully submitted,

CALVIN TOMKINS,
Commissioner of Docks.

www.ingramcontent.com/pod-product-compliance
Lightning Source LLC
LaVergne TN
LVHW020633110826
845149LV00004B/1162

* 9 7 8 1 4 1 8 1 8 6 6 5 4 *